CONCRETE
Garden Projects

EASY & INEXPENSIVE
CONTAINERS, FURNITURE,
WATER FEATURES
& MORE

Malin Nilsson
Camilla Arvidsson

Timber Press
Portland • London

For our
children

August

Jack

Kalle

Ellen

Originally published as *Vattenblänk & Betong*
© 2010 Ica Bokförlag, Forma Books AB. All rights reserved.

This edition published in 2011 © Timber Press, Inc.

The Haseltine Building
133 S.W. Second Avenue, Suite 450
Portland, Oregon 97204-3527
www.timberpress.com

2 The Quadrant
135 Salusbury Road
London NW6 6RJ
www.timberpress.co.uk

ISBN-13: 978-1-60469-282-2

Printed in China

Catalogue records for this book are available from the
Library of Congress and the British Library.

CONCRETE GARDEN PROJECTS

Contents

Hooray for concrete!

Concrete is a magical material that can produce sober, heavy-weight pots one minute and delicate, fragile leaf prints the next. More and more people are discovering what a fantastic material concrete can be in the garden, with rough concrete providing an excellent foil for greenery. Water is another great complement to it, whether it be as a birdbath sunk into a dazzling flowerbed, or a small pond complete with a trickling fountain. On the other hand, weathering by the wind and rain imbues it with a dignified, aged look and encourages moss to develop, making the object even more beautiful.

We have been using concrete as a medium for years, but are still constantly surprised by its potential, which often gives rise to new ideas. This book is a collection of our favourite projects, large and small: pots, birdbaths, tealight holders, stepping stones, a barbecue-cum-outdoor-kitchen, and much, much more. We have also chosen to include in the book inspirational images of finished concrete objects in our own gardens.

Once you have selected a project, follow the detailed, step-by-step instructions provided in the project handbook at the back of the book. We hope that those of you who have worked with concrete before will find something new to try and that newcomers will be inspired to give it a go—it's really not as difficult as you might think. Good luck!

Martin Camilla

Numbers show the way

There are a variety of moulds you can use to create attractive house numbers. Our preferred one for this project is a number from a giant foam floor puzzle. These are available in a variety of sizes from most toy shops. Puzzle pieces like this make great moulds, and the end results are consistent and attractive.

Styrofoam is an ideal alternative if you want to make your own number templates. As styrofoam is available in various thicknesses, you can make the number as big and/or thick as you like. A similar template could also be used to stamp the number down into a square of wet concrete.

You can also take this project a step further by decorating the number with some pretty pebbles or mosaic tiles. Or why not paint it? Dots could be fun!

This concrete number has been hung on a gate using a nail.
★ *Full instructions on page 102.*

Come on in!

Whether you work or play in the garden, a shoe scraper is great for getting mud off shoes and makes an attractive feature in itself. Use pieces of triangular moulding that have been nailed to a sheet of plywood to create the raised edges.

Concrete scrapers are durable and weatherproof. Any mud and dirt on them will be washed off by the rain, but they will also withstand a once-over with the hose if necessary.

Make your home more inviting by arranging plants in a variety of pots on your steps, like the miniature rose, thyme and common box seen here. A good tip is to always keep some winter greenery to hand so that it can be supplemented with seasonal blooms to give a warm welcome all year round. If your steps have railings, you could also try winding some evergreen ivy around them.

This shoe scraper has been laid in gravel at the foot of some steps.
✱ *Full instructions on page 103.*

Timeless pots

Concrete pots are beautiful all year round. They look fantastic planted with geraniums in summer, asters in autumn and Christmas roses in winter. That said, it's hard to beat a display of potted spring bulbs. If you buy forced ones, you can even enjoy some early spring colour.

One of the easiest—and prettiest—things you can make out of concrete is a small pot. Gently rounded, straight-sided or even star-shaped—you decide. Kitchen containers and plastic pots make excellent moulds. Plastic bottles are handy for making the hollow inside the pot. Make each pot unique by varying the thickness of the walls and the shape of the inside of the pot. A square pot can have a round inside and vice versa. Remember that the pots do not all need to be the same height—ones that are short and wide mixed with ones that are tall and thin will make an attractive display.

Set a spring table with pots of different shapes and sizes. This concrete tabletop is resting on an old wrought-iron table.
✱ *Full instructions on pages 104 and 119.*

During the construction process, you can make one or more drainage holes in the base of the pot using a cork or piece of styrofoam to allow any excess water to drain away. For pots without holes, put a layer of clay balls in the bottom before filling the pot with compost to help absorb excess water and to combat root rot.

Then gather together a number of different pots or choose
one in which to plant your favourite flowers. Set a spring table
that is pleasing to the eye, with sky-blue grape hyacinths,
scented hyacinths, crocus buds and elegant Christmas roses
with their long-lasting blooms. Nothing beats the first show of
spring colour.

A collection of pots cast using a variety of moulds. Concrete is darker when
wet and lightens as it dries. ✶ *Full instructions on page 104.*

Vintage garden furniture sets off spring blooms displayed in various concrete pots. The tabletop is made of concrete and its weight keeps the structure stable. The old plum tree in the background is covered in ivy.

Try making the inside of the pot a different shape—pretty bulbs can be left uncovered, or soil can be covered with small stones.

✶ *Full instructions on pages 104 and 119.*

Decorative edges

It takes next to no time to decorate the rims of pots for added effect. One idea is to use a piece of oiled, soft cord or string to make a serpentine pattern in the wet concrete. Once the concrete has set, remove the cord or string to reveal an elegant relief.

The pot shown here was cast in a large, round, plastic bucket, while the interior was created using a square container. As the inside is quite small in relation to the pot as a whole, its walls and top edges are fairly thick, allowing plenty of space for a decorative pattern. Experiment by varying the thicknesses of your cord or rope, which can create quite a different end result.

Mosaic tiles or glass pebbles set into and around the edge of the pot also make an attractive alternative. Go dotty by pressing oiled corks into the wet concrete. Or why not try variously patterned stamps? There are plenty of options—play around and find your favourite.

A piece of oiled cord was used here to create a pretty edge pattern.
★ *Full instructions on page 105.*

Larger pots

Casting large pots requires a little more work, but these make a practical and attractive home for perennial plants. Add a little fertilizer and water and they virtually look after themselves, and there is plenty of room for roots to develop.

Large, square pots, like those shown overleaf, are best cast in home-made moulds. Film-faced plywood is great for making square and rectangular moulds. It has a smooth surface and does not absorb water, so the concrete will not stick to the mould.

Screw the mould together to ensure it is sufficiently sturdy. You will need two different moulds: a large one for the outside walls and a smaller one for the interior ones. The gap between them depends on how thick you would like the walls to be. Our larger pots generally have walls that are about 5 cm (2 in.) thick.

Some large pots, however, may need reinforcing. If this is the case, make sure that the reinforcement is not visible. Use a piece

A large, round pot contains easy-care ribbon grass and the wall behind supports a large, flowering white clematis. Overleaf: Imposing square pots contain ribbon grass and common box.

✶ *Full instructions on pages 111 and 106.*

of styrofoam or a small, plastic pot to make a drainage hole in the base.

Use a concrete form tube, available in different sizes from builders' merchants and other suppliers, or two large, plastic pots to make a cylindrical pot—then follow the process on page 111.

It can be a good idea to attach wheels to large heavy pots, so they can be moved without you having to pick them up. Remember that if you want to embed the wheels in the concrete, you have to cast the pot upside down and incorporate a base plate. This can be tricky, but it is possible. However, it is easier to attach wheels to the finished pot using construction adhesive.

Large, freshly cast pots are at risk of cracking if they dry too quickly. To avoid this and help the concrete dry more slowly, spray the pot with water for the first few days. A really big pot will need to cure for four to five days, so be patient.

A large, round pot, with a dotted rim produced with corks, has been planted with lush thyme. ✱ *Full instructions on page 107.*

Natural wear

You will notice that as concrete begins to become weathered, moss will start to grow on it. If you would like to give nature a helping hand and speed up the weathering process, try adding one part peat to three parts concrete mix when casting. The resulting mix is called hypertufa. The peat makes the concrete more porous, enabling moss and lichen to gain a hold quickly. The more peat you add, the sooner you will get moss-covered pots. However, too much peat can make the pot brittle and more inclined to break, so it's important to get the mix just right.

You can also speed up the growth of moss and lichen by brushing the finished pot with soured milk or yoghurt mixed with a little soil. This will encourage an even faster rate of growth.

A simple pot made of concrete mixed with peat gives the impression of being aged and weathered. This hosta almost looks as if it is a part of the pot. ✶ *Full instructions on pages 106 and 108.*

If you want to accentuate an aged effect, try casting pots in cardboard boxes, so that the shape is not perfect, but slightly softer and more characterful.

The weathered appearance of this type of concrete enables pots to blend into their surroundings. A surface with a good covering of lichen and moss is reminiscent of natural stone. In fact, once in situ the pot will look as though it has been in the garden for years, making it the ideal choice for a wild border or as a complement to other slightly rusted garden ornaments.

Hypertufa is also great for making small decorative features, such as small balls or hearts, which you can shape using your gloved hands.

A rusted, water-filled dish with a heart and balls made from hypertufa as a centrepiece makes a beautiful still life. A houseleek is growing in the pot. ✶ *Full instructions on page 108.*

Stepping stones

Heavy-duty cardboard tubes are extremely useful when it comes to casting concrete. These are available in different lengths and diameters from builders' merchants and DIY stores. When sawn into a lot of smaller moulds that are approximately 5 cm (2 in.) high, they are perfect for casting round stepping stones.

Lay the sawn sections of tube on a flat surface (a sheet of chipboard is good). Oil both the moulds and the surface before pouring in the concrete, allowing you to make a lot of stepping stones at the same time.

You might also like to create patterns on some and alternate these with plain, smooth stepping stones in your path. Create attractive impressions on the surface using scroll-

Round stepping stones form a secret path through this woodland area.
★ *Full instructions on page 109.*

patterned doormats, rubber underlay, thick cords or textured leaves. Don't forget to oil the pattern mould well before using it.

You can also cast birdbaths the same size as the stepping stones to include along the path. The moulds should be the same shape and size as those used for the stepping stones. Use a plastic lid or similar to make the hollow in the middle of the bath.

Arrange the finished stepping stones to form a path through the garden. Lay them in gravel or on the lawn, or why not create a secret path through a wilderness with them?

Three different ideas for stepping stones.
★ *Full instructions on pages 109 and 120.*

Growing on through

Concrete slabs look completely different with holes in them, through which small flowers can grow. It is even possible to cast such slabs to be used on a terrace, with their holes being perfect for low-growing plants, such as thyme.

Measure out the size that you would like your slab to be and fashion a mould of the same size. For optimum results, make your own mould using film-faced plywood and timber battens screwed together. This should make the mould easy to dismantle once the slab has set, so it can be used multiple times.

We have used a round plastic container for the hole in the middle, but you can use anything you like.

A slab laid on the lawn with blue squill.
✱ *Full instructions on page 110.*

Miniature ponds

The gentle murmur of water encourages relaxation and creates a tranquil atmosphere in the garden. Even a small pond, like the one shown here, can be heavy and should therefore be reinforced during the casting process to make it more durable and to prevent it cracking. Try reinforcing your project with mesh or rods, although chicken wire also works well. Be sure to cover the mesh or wire with plenty of concrete so that it is concealed inside and out.

We cast our pond using large plastic tubs. To ensure that the walls are sufficiently thick, use two different sizes of tub, with one able to fit inside the other.

The cable for the pump can hang over the edge and be concealed by surrounding plants. However, it will look better if you drill a hole for the cable in the side of the pot and then seal the

A pond with a water pump conjures up images of a fountain. Overleaf: Pond with aquatic iris. Around it are hostas, roses and French lavender in pots. Ornaments like the frog can be found at almost any garden centre.
✱ *Full instructions on page 111.*

hole around the cable with silicone. Leave the sealant to dry before filling your pond with water. If you want to take the pump out and need to remove the cable, cut the sealant away from the hole before removing it and apply a fresh coating of sealant over the hole when you replace the cable.

A miniature pond is a good home for fish, especially goldfish, though choosing a suitable pump for your fish-filled pond is also important. A large DIY store or garden centre will stock a wide range of pumps. Remember also that you may wish to move the fish somewhere else over winter, as small ponds can freeze solid if they get cold enough.

Pond plants, such as aquatic irises and water lilies, do well in these environments. Put stones on the bottom to give their roots something to cling to, and arrange greenery and flowering plants in pots around the pond to create a miniature oasis.

Water feature with pump amidst ivy and lavender—simple yet beautiful!
★ *Full instructions on page 107.*

Barbecue-cum-outdoor-kitchen

What are warm summer evenings for if not cooking outdoors? A concrete bench can double as an outdoor kitchen, providing plenty of space for food preparation and a few ornamental pots.

If you are new to the medium of concrete, this is probably not the best project to start with—although it is not as difficult as it looks. All you need is a good solid mould for casting. Once your unit is fully assembled, you will be able to enjoy evening barbecues for many years to come.

When making the bench, form a round hole in it for a kettle barbecue. The walls supporting this bench are made from blocks of LECA (Lightweight Expanded Clay Aggregate) that have been plastered and painted.

The concrete bench can stay outside over the winter; only the barbecue needs to come inside.

This barbecue bench provides a practical work surface and an attractive table for a summer buffet.

★ *Full instructions on page 112.*

Arrange pretty bowls and pots of herbs and other plants on top of your
bench. Here we have an olive tree and a small pot of cotton lavender.
✴ *Full instructions on pages 112 and 113.*

Decorative ideas

Patterns and shapes can have a big impact when working with concrete, as they're able to make any project into something special. Keep napkins tidy with a concrete shell you've created, or try making an unusual, starfish-shaped dish.

Sand moulds are great for casting concrete, as they are decorative and easy to use, and arts and crafts shops and home furnishing stores also stock a good range of items that can be used as moulds. You don't necessarily have to buy something new though—your own home can be a treasure trove. Take a look around and see what you can find to use for casting concrete. Look for objects with internal and external patterns and embellishments, as new design ideas are all around us.

Silicone bakeware is especially good for casting concrete,

The shell (top left) and flower (bottom right) were cast in the same way, using different sand moulds, while the starfish dish features an impression from a sand mould. A small glass flower adorns the bottom of the birdbath.
★ *Full instructions on pages 128 (for the shell and flower), 113 and 114.*

and there is plenty of it to choose from these days. Silicone moulds are extremely easy to use, as they stretch and are easy to remove once the concrete has set.

Try adding different materials to the concrete for an attractive contrast. With so many mosaic tiles and glass decorations around, the possibilities are endless. Visit your local arts and crafts shop or tile supplier and remember to ask if they have any offcuts or broken tiles you can have.

For example, why not embed glass pendants or mirror tiles as a decorative feature in the bottom of a bowl? Fill it with water to make a birdbath with added pizzazz. Pearl beads, pendants and mirrored objects reflect light, giving off a very pleasing effect. Pretty shells and stones you have collected also work

Birdbath with small mirrors embedded in the bottom. The mirrors were originally Christmas decorations.
★ *Full instructions on page 114.*

really well. Trawl flea markets for old, odd pieces of porcelain to smash up and use to create your own mosaics.

How much decoration you add is entirely up to you: you could cover the whole birdbath with a mosaic, just decorate the bottom of the bowl or add edging around the rim. Create a meandering pattern with beads, write a message in pebbles or place a single small mirror in the bottom of the birdbath to capture and reflect light.

It is also effective to cast small, decorative objects to stand on the rim of a birdbath. Let your imagination run wild and try out different methods until you are happy with the results.

Birdbath with edge inlaid with round, white mosaic tiles, a hand-made heart and pieces of limestone. To give the impression that the birdbath and pots are floating, stand them on spacer blocks. This also helps protect your wooden decking.

★ *Full instructions on page 118.*

Adding colour

It is possible to obtain concrete dyes, but we think that to achieve the best results you need to get painting. Choose between painting the entire surface, just adding details, adding stripes and dots, or using templates.

Ready-to-use stencils that are available from arts and crafts shops and DIY stores are easy to use, but why not create your own with masking tape or double-sided tape? Simply place the stencil over the concrete and apply spray paint in your chosen colour. It is a good idea to use silicate paint on concrete, but normal enamel paint also works well. Enamel paints are a little more vulnerable to the wind and weather, which means the paint will need retouching at some point. Paint delicate patterns on birdbaths and pots or decorate small, useful stools with various patterns. The stools overleaf are about 30 cm (12 in.) tall and were cast using plain, plastic buckets.

A small birdbath with stencilled flowers. We used a large ball to make the actual bath. Overleaf: Small stools in a variety of patterns among lilac bowers. ✳ *Full instructions on pages 119 and 115.*

Natural impressions

There is a lot of beauty in nature, and forests provide a wealth of material for making impressions in concrete, like interesting leaves, twigs or any other foliage. Leaves from hostas, hollyhocks and maple trees make great stamps. Simple tiles like the ones with a leaf print here (these leaves were picked from a garden) will look good leaning against a tree, a fence or a shed wall. Place them in a flowerbed for plants to grow around them or try laying the tile flat and filling the leaf impression with water to make a small garden mirror.

To make these leaf impressions, we rubbed our leaves with oil, placed them underside down on the wet concrete (to ensure that the veins would show up clearly), and weighed them down with some pebbles, which help to press the leaf into the concrete. The impression is then clearer and slightly indented.

Pretty concrete tablets with impressions of hosta, hollyhock, ivy and elm leaves surrounded by greenery.
★ *Full instructions on page 116.*

To make dishes or birdbaths in the shape of a leaf, it is best to build your own mould out of grit or coarse sand. Find a flat, level surface and make a pile of grit or sand about the same size and shape as your preferred leaf. Moisten the grit or sand with water so that it holds together. Oil the leaf and lay it underside up on the mound of sand or grit, then pour the concrete carefully onto the leaf to make a 'dish' of the required thickness.

For birdbaths, use large leaves from plants such as rhubarb or thistle. For smaller dishes, try leaves from hostas, hollyhocks, lady's mantle or coral flower.

This technique can also be useful for casting plain dishes and birdbaths. Using grit or sand as a mould will give the concrete a slightly rougher, more textured finish. Don't worry if any sand or grit sticks to the concrete, as it can be brushed off later.

Nature provides some of the prettiest moulds, like this one from a giant hosta.
★ *Full instructions on page 117.*

Practical planting bench

A planting bench in a quiet corner of the garden with storage for pots and containers makes gardening even more enjoyable. Benches are ideal surfaces on which to sow seeds, transfer seedlings into pots, and tie bouquets of seasonal blooms and foliage from your garden, with your favourite tools always to hand.

Here we have cast some concrete shelves that require absolutely no maintenance and can withstand the vagaries of the changing seasons. The shelves are attached to a wooden wall that has been painted grey. They are quite heavy, so always remember to use sturdy brackets.

Cast your shelves in a mould built using timber battens and film-faced plywood. It is important that you reinforce your shelves to ensure stability.

Concrete shelves with pottery. Leave pots and tools on show, ready for use. The top shelf is made from an old windowsill. Overleaf: Another concrete shelf with a late summer bouquet of white Japanese anemones and aster buds with white pots planted with ornamental cabbage.
★ *Full instructions on page 112.*

Water features and birdbaths

A birdbath is a simple way to add a small water feature to your garden. Think of it almost as a garden mirror. Experiment with different moulds and think about areas of your garden where birds might like to take a dip.

Birdbaths can be large or small, square or round, flat or slightly deeper like small bowls. Place these little mirrors on the lawn, amidst a carpet of lilies, in the shadow of a tree or under a beautiful rose bush, so that falling petals land and float on the surface of the water.

Birdbaths are not difficult to make—it's just like casting a pot. Larger ones can be a bit trickier, so take extra care when lifting a large, freshly cast bath to ensure it does not crack.

Large, round plastic basins or square tubs make excellent moulds, but you can just as easily make your own using sheet

A large bowl makes an elegant birdbath for this balcony, with the railings supporting a Chinese wisteria.
★ *Full instructions on page 107.*

Birdbaths of all shapes and sizes can enhance a garden. Opposite: A birdbath
set among hostas and lady's mantle.

✱ *Full instructions on pages 120, 118 and 119.*

plywood and timber battens. A little carpentry is required here, but it is not difficult.

For a round birdbath, you will need two heavy-duty cardboard tubes of different diameters (available from builders' merchants and other suppliers). Saw the tubes off at your preferred length and place them on a flat surface, which will act as the base for the mould. This method can also be used to cast pots.

You can never have too many birdbaths—fill any simple dish with water and you have one! Remember to top them up with a watering can now and again, as shallower ones will dry up more quickly.

A simple, understated birdbath supported by cobblestones, with a floating white clematis flower.
★ *Full instructions on page 118.*

Roses and romance

The slightly rough finish of concrete makes it an excellent material to use when making roses and other romantic elements in a garden. These roses were cast using silicone muffin cases. Silicone moulds stretch and are easy to remove once the concrete has hardened, making these roses some of the easiest items you can cast in concrete and a perfect project for beginners.

There are numerous heart-shaped moulds available in the form of cake tins, sand moulds and cookie cutters, but if you cannot find anything suitable, you can easily make your own out of styrofoam. Simply sketch your heart design on to the styrofoam and cut it out.

Small roses and hearts also look just as good inside as they do outside. In the house, use them as napkin weights, decorative ornaments on windowsills or next to your front door. Why not give a heart or roses as a gift to someone you care about?

Roses in an old, water-filled zinc dish.
★ *Full instructions on page 121.*

Opposite: Birdbath with a small heart relief. Above: A selection of simple
hearts. Below: A heart and some rose petals.

✳ *Full instructions on pages 124, 128, 122 and 123.*

A quiet corner

A concrete bench is a durable piece of garden furniture that can stay outside all year round. You can make your own mould using timber battens and film-faced plywood for a stylish and sturdy concrete bench. Screw the mould together to make it easy to dismantle once the concrete has set. To reuse the mould, simply reassemble it when required.

The bench in the picture is 115 cm (46 in.) long, 30 cm (12 in.) wide and 45 cm (18 in.) high. It is quite heavy to move, but very stable once in position.

When positioning your bench in the garden, preferably place it against a wall or a hedge, where you can relax, unwind and take in the pleasant view. Why not add a soft cushion to make the seat more comfortable? A concrete bench can also be a practical and attractive feature to have indoors or in a greenhouse.

Bench with potted daylily and a pretty little dish. Overleaf: A peaceful garden sanctuary with a white pot planted with African white lily in front of some ribbon grass.
★ *Full instructions on pages 125, 105 and 113.*

Tealight holders

Candles are always beautiful. Nothing beats sitting outside on a quiet summer evening watching candles flicker on your garden table, or welcoming visitors in winter with a glowing candle out on your front steps.

Small candle and tealight holders are easy to make and are a good project for beginners not used to working with concrete. Try using a variety of moulds, such as silicone muffin cases or small plastic containers, like empty sour cream tubs.

Oil your candle first before pressing it into the filled mould, then leave the candle in the concrete as it sets—you'll be able to remove it later, but don't forget to wash the oil off the candle before lighting it.

Here are some simple tealight holders that were made using silicone muffin cases. Overleaf: Top your garden table with various candleholders and decorate with daisies.
★ *Full instructions on page 126.*

Small bowls also make good candleholders. Fill pretty concrete bowls with water and decorate with floating candles and flowers. Place block candles in slightly larger, shallow dishes and cover with a hurricane lamp glass to protect their flames. ✳ *Full instructions on pages 114 and 104.*

Fun with shapes

Silicone ice cube trays come in a variety of shapes and sizes and are fantastic for casting concrete. It is possible to cast a lot of small shapes at the same time using only a small amount of mix. These little objects have many uses: as tablecloth weights, pot stands, napkin holders, candleholders or even just as decorations. We have used some with holes in them as incense stick holders and have attached wire to others to make hanging garden ornaments.

You could even play board games using the shapes as pieces, as a simple square slab can easily be turned into a noughts and crosses, or tic-tac-toe, board. Once the slab has set, mark out squares with masking tape, spray the slab with paint and remove the tape for a board you can leave out all year round.

Pretty little incense stick holders in a shallow zinc dish.
★ *Full instructions on page 127.*

Opposite: A hanging garden ornament made using wire, ice cube shapes and a glass pendant. Above: A simple noughts and crosses, or tic-tac-toe, set.

✶ *Full instructions on page 127.*

Flowery cakes

Throw a garden party and surprise guests with these unusual cakes, which are a treat for the senses in terms of colour and shape.

Dig out some cake tins and sand moulds to create a wonderful still life in concrete that you can decorate with fresh flowers. One idea is to arrange a cake covered in flowers, or several such cakes, on a small table beside the buffet. Use different moulds of various sizes to give the display added effect.

Alternatively, place the cakes in a dish of water and pack flowers tightly around the edge. Make use of bold colours or uniformly pale blooms. The blooms will last surprisingly well outdoors.

This is a simple yet fun project that encourages playfulness and creative zest.

Get casting!

This colourful garden table is a feast to behold and an amusing alternative to vases of flowers.

✱ *Full instructions on page 128.*

Cakes with flowers packed around the edge are fun and easy to make, and a little water in the hole in the middle is an elegant touch too. Choose seasonal blooms to complement them. We have used asters and dahlias here.

✱ *Full instructions on page 128.*

Guardian angels

When winter arrives, the atmosphere in a garden is almost magical. Small, frost-covered cherubs by the front door can bid you and your guests a warm welcome. Concrete withstands cold well and is beautifully set off by an ethereal dusting of frost. Prolonged exposure to unusually harsh weather can cause the angels' features to become roughened, which often only adds to their beauty.

A zinc stake pushed into the setting concrete will allow the finished angel to be used in a border or a pot. They also make elegant reliefs for concrete tiles, especially if painted silver or gold.

Art and craft shops sell a variety of moulds for casting angels and cherubs, although it is possible to make your own from a porcelain figurine. To do this, apply several coats of silicone rubber (available from larger art and craft suppliers) to the

A frost-covered cherub slumbers peacefully.
★ *Full instructions on page 129.*

Opposite: Group angels or cherubs together with concrete and zinc pots.
Hang eye-catching glass pendants from corkscrew hazel for added effect.
Above: Cherubs on stakes in a zinc pot of common box. Below: An attractive
concrete tile with angel impression on gravel.

✱ *Full instructions on page 129, 130, 104 and 114.*

figurine with a brush. Once the silicone has set, remove it from the figurine and fill your silicone mould with concrete. If using this method, you will find that small porcelain or plastic figurines work best because of their solid, slightly glossy surfaces.

A small angel will sit happily and peacefully in a bowl of water, like a guardian angel. Put some green moss around the bowl to soften the effect and bring some additional colour to the concrete. Float some houseleeks in the water like water lilies. Snowfall will make the scene even more beautiful.

Stand an angel in a small bowl of water with some floating houseleeks and decorate all around with moss.

★ *Full instructions on pages 131 and 104.*

PROJECT HANDBOOK

Working with concrete

Concrete has a long history. The Romans used it to build amphitheatres, viaducts and aqueducts. It's said that concrete sets over one hundred years, remains still for one hundred years and slowly begins to weather after another hundred years. Concrete is a natural material, which is comprised of ballast (a stabilizing material such as stone, gravel or sand), cement and water.

There are many different types of concrete. We have used fine concrete for the projects in this book, which we feel produces the best result. For a smoother finish, try repair mortar or repair concrete. For a rougher finish, choose coarse concrete. Grain size makes all the difference when it comes to concrete. The smaller the grain, the smoother the concrete.

The easiest way to begin making concrete for casting is to buy ready-mixed, dry concrete, to which you just need to add water. Ready-mixed, dry concrete is available in 25 kg (55 lbs) bags from builders' merchants and other suppliers. One bag of dry concrete mixed with approximately four litres (one gallon) of water will make about 13 litres (3¼ gallons) of concrete. Adding less water will produce a stronger mix, but make sure that the consistency is loose enough to work with. The consistency is usually about right if you can roll a ball that holds its shape and the size of a small bun with the mix.

Making your own concrete can be a bit tricky, but it is possible. Mix three parts ballast with one part cement and add water until the consistency is right.

Remember to fill moulds somewhere where splashes of the concrete mix and dust won't matter, as the former can be pretty sticky. Out in the garden or on your balcony is a good idea. Put a sheet of wood or plastic down as a protective surface. Concrete is also corrosive, so be sure to wear protective gloves. Ordinary washing up gloves are good, as they are elastic and you can feel the material through them. You can work without gloves if you avoid direct contact with the concrete, but wash your hands thoroughly afterwards. Concrete can be cast all year round, but bear in mind that in very cold weather the water in wet concrete can freeze, making the concrete split.

Mix your concrete in a large bucket or tub. If mixing a small amount, it is a good idea to use a trowel or a large spatula. For larger projects, it is easier to use a mixer. Mixers and stirrers that can be attached to a drill or a powered screwdriver are available. Only mix as much concrete as you need. You can always mix up some more if required, which is better than mixing too much.

There is no shortage of moulds around. Rummage around the house or look round flea markets and shops if you need ideas. Old plastic buckets, bowls and tubs all make good, basic moulds. Once you have chosen your mould, oil it well to prevent the concrete from sticking as it sets. Ordinary cooking oil works brilliantly, but mould oil is also available from builders' merchants if you prefer it. When filling the mould, make sure you pack the mix down well and shake and tap the filled mould to get rid of any air bubbles, ensuring a smooth surface.

Large objects that will be exposed to the elements need to be reinforced. For best results, use chicken wire, reinforcing rods or mesh.

To finish, leave the concrete to harden. This requires a little patience, as you don't want to remove the mould too soon. Drying times vary depending on the size of the object, but give any project at least 24 hours to harden. Spritz larger items with a little water using a hand spray and cover them with plastic to prevent them drying too quickly, which can lead to cracking. Don't leave objects to dry in direct sunlight or very shady areas.

Detailed step-by-step instructions for all the projects shown in this book are provided on the following pages. Good luck!

Large, charming numbers for attaching to walls or fences are easy to make using pieces from a numerical foam floor puzzle as moulds. Use a piece of board as a base for the mould during casting. The same method can also be used to make letters, using pieces of an alphabetical foam floor puzzle as moulds.

YOU WILL NEED: fine concrete, foam floor puzzle pieces, a piece of board, oil, a paintbrush, a spatula, weights and a file.

1. Begin by oiling the board and the edges of the puzzle piece with the paintbrush.

2. Place a few weights on the mould to keep it from moving, then mix the concrete and fill the mould.

3. Level the surface with a spatula, leaving it smooth and neat.

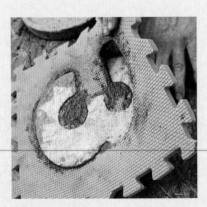

4. Leave the concrete to set for 24 to 48 hours, depending on the size of your number, then carefully remove the mould.

5. Smooth away any sharp edges with a stone or a file.

6. Hang the number on a nail or stand it on a small shelf against a fence or house wall.

Making a shoe scraper

This practical, attractive and, most importantly, durable shoe scraper is quite easy to make. A little carpentry is required to produce a good mould, but on the plus side, you can always reuse it. It is important to reinforce the concrete used here, as this item will see a lot of use.

YOU WILL NEED: fine concrete, film-faced plywood, timber battens, some triangular moulding, brads (small headless nails), screws, mesh for reinforcement, oil, a paintbrush and a wide spatula.

1. Cut and assemble the parts for the mould. We used film-faced plywood, 4 timber battens and 8 pieces of triangular moulding. Nail the triangular moulding to the plywood using brads.

2. Screw the battens together at the mould's edges, so they are easy to remove later on. Oil the entire mould.

3. Once the mould is ready, mix the concrete. Apply a thin layer using the spatula.

4. Add the reinforcing mesh and top up with more concrete. Skim the surface with the spatula to level it.

5. Leave the concrete to set for a week and spritz it with water a few times to stop it drying out too quickly. Covering it with plastic can help to keep it damp for longer. Remove the mould.

6. A finished shoe scraper.

Making a small pot or a bowl

Small pots and bowls are easy to make and you can vary their design as much as you like by using different interior and exterior moulds, as concrete will reflect the patterns or stripes in any mould. A fluted plastic pot is ideal for making similarly shaped concrete ones.

YOU WILL NEED: fine concrete, two different sized plastic pots or containers, oil, a paintbrush, a spatula, a weight and a stone or a file.

1. Begin by oiling the inside of the larger (exterior) mould, taking extra care when using a fluted mould.

2. Oil the outside of the smaller (interior) mould.

3. Mix the concrete and fill the larger mould with concrete up to about 2 cm (1 in.) from the top. This will stop the concrete from overflowing when you add the smaller mould.

4. Shake the larger mould with the concrete in it to get rid of any air bubbles and to level the surface of the concrete, then press the second, smaller mould into the middle of the larger one. Don't press it down too far or else the base will be too thin.

5. Put a weight in the empty, smaller mould to stop it rising. Leave to set.

6. Wait 24 to 48 hours, depending on the size of the pot. Carefully remove the moulds and to finish, smooth away any sharp edges with a stone or a file.

Making a pot with a serpentine pattern

A piece of cord, whether it be thick or thin, can leave a wonderful impression in concrete. In this project, we snaked and twirled a piece of cord around the rim of a thick pot. Why not add a similar design to the bottom of a birdbath? For this pot, we used a large round bowl and a square container as moulds.

YOU WILL NEED: fine concrete, two different sized bowls or containers, a piece of cord, oil, a paintbrush, a trowel, a weight, a stone or a file and a masonry drill bit (optional).

1. Begin by oiling the inside of the larger mould and the outside of the smaller one.

2. Thoroughly oil the cord. Use gloves if you don't want greasy fingers.

3. Mix the concrete and fill the larger mould, leaving 2 cm (1 in.) free at the top. Shake the bowl to get rid of any air bubbles and to level the surface.

4. Press the smaller container into the middle of the larger one. Remember not to press it down too much or the base will be too thin. Put a weight in the smaller mould to keep it in place.

5. Arrange the cord in an attractive pattern in the concrete between the moulds and press it down gently. Leave the concrete to set for 48 hours.

6. Carefully remove the cord and moulds. Smooth away any sharp edges with a stone or a file. Use a masonry drill bit to make drainage holes in the base of the pot, if desired.

Part of this project involves building a mould—ours is made from sturdy film-faced plywood. Use this method to cast really big pots, which require interior and exterior moulds. No base is required; just stand them on a piece of board.

Remember to put the timber battens on the outside of the exterior mould, making unscrewing the mould easier. These moulds can also be reused.

YOU WILL NEED: fine concrete, film-faced plywood, timber battens, boards, screws, mesh for reinforcement, oil, a paintbrush, a spatula or trowel, a small plastic pot, gloves and a stone or a file.

1. Measure out the dimensions for your pot and cut your battens and boards to size. Assemble them into moulds using screws, then cut your reinforcing mesh or rods to size. Oil the moulds.

2. Mix the concrete and put a small, oiled, plastic pot in the bottom to make a drainage hole. Fill the base with concrete in a layer about 5 cm (2 in.) thick and pack down.

3. Position the interior mould on top of the wet concrete. If necessary, you can nail pieces of wood right across the two moulds to keep them in place. Press the reinforcing mesh or rods vertically in between the two moulds.

4. Fill the remaining space with concrete. Tamp or flatten the concrete down with a piece of timber to get rid of any air bubbles.

5. Leave the concrete to set for two days. Remove the moulds and spray the concrete with water to stop it drying out too quickly. Leave to stand for a couple more days.

6. To finish, smooth away any sharp edges with a stone or file and get planting!

Making a round, large pot or bowl

Use two solid moulds for slightly larger bowls or pots. Normal plastic bowls are great, but remember to vary the appearance and size of your projects by using different moulds. We made this pot without a drainage hole, but we recommend you make one for really large pots. To do this, put a piece of styrofoam or a cork in the bottom of your larger mould, before adding the concrete.

YOU WILL NEED: fine concrete, two different sized bowls, a weight, oil, a paintbrush, a trowel and a stone or a file.

1. Begin by oiling the inside of the larger bowl and the outside of the smaller one.

2. Mix the concrete and fill the larger mould with it to just below the top. This will stop the concrete from overflowing when you add the smaller mould.

3. Shake the bowl to get rid of any air bubbles and to level the concrete's surface.

4. Press the smaller bowl into the middle of the larger one. Remember not to press it down too much, or the base will become too thin. Put a weight in the smaller bowl to keep it in place.

5. Leave the bowl to set for 48 to 72 hours, depending on its size. Carefully remove the moulds.

6. Smooth away any sharp edges with a stone or a file.

Hypertufa is made by adding one part peat to three parts concrete mix. When the consistency is right, a small ball of the mix should hold its shape, but the more peat you add, the more brittle the object becomes, altering the surface texture of the concrete and encouraging moss and lichen to take hold. This mixture also makes fantastic pots.

YOU WILL NEED: fine concrete, peat, a piece of board, a trowel and gloves.

1. Begin by mixing the concrete and adding the required amount of peat.

2. Mix the concrete well, adding more water or peat as required.

3. Try rolling the mixture into a ball to see if it holds its shape.

4. Use your gloved hands to mould balls, spheres or other interesting shapes of various sizes.

5. Shape one of the balls into a heart with your gloved hands. The easiest way to do this is on a flat surface.

6. This mixture will take longer to set than usual (about a week) because the peat will retain moisture for longer.

Making a stepping stone

Casting stepping stones using cardboard tubes is easy, as there is no need to build a mould, and you can also make multiple casts at the same time if you wish. Cardboard tubes are available in different sizes from builders' merchants and other suppliers. We used tubes that were 25 cm (10 in.) in diameter here. We used pieces of a rubber doormat to produce beautiful scroll patterns on the stones.

YOU WILL NEED: fine concrete, cardboard tubing, pieces of rubber doormat, a piece of board, a saw, a ruler, oil, a paintbrush, a trowel and a stone or a file.

1. Begin by sawing the tube into rings that are 5 cm (2 in.) high, then trim your piece of rubber doormat to fit inside the cardboard ring.

2. Place the rings on your piece of board. Oil the rings and the board.

3. Mix the concrete and fill the moulds, skimming off the excess when done. Shake the mould gently to distribute the concrete evenly and to get rid of any air bubbles. Oil your trimmed piece of rubber doormat.

4. Press the rubber mat evenly into the concrete. If you are casting more than one stone, keep some of your others plain to vary your pattern. Leave to set.

5. After 48 hours and if the concrete has set, carefully remove the piece of rubber doormat.

6. Gently ease the cardboard rings off the stones. These rings can be reused if you would like to make more stepping stones at another time. Smooth away any sharp edges with a stone or a file.

To make this slab, you will need to build a mould out of plywood or film-faced plywood and timber battens. You can make one with a rectangular or a square shape, or with one hole or multiple holes. You can also use a square object to make a square hole if you prefer. We went for a square slab with a round hole. Your hole can be filled with stones, flowers or anything else you like.

YOU WILL NEED: fine concrete, timber battens, plywood or film-faced plywood, screws, a bowl or a container to make the hole with, oil, a paintbrush and a trowel.

1. Begin by screwing your timber battens to your plywood or film-faced plywood board. We made this mould using timber battens and a sheet of plywood cut to measure 30 cm × 30 cm (12 in. × 12 in.).

2. Oil the entire mould, as well as the bowl or container you will use to make the hole.

3. Mix the concrete, then position your bowl or container upside down where you would like the hole to be and pour the concrete in around it. Use a weight to stop the bowl from moving.

4. Level the surface with a trowel or a spatula.

5. Leave to set for 3 days before carefully removing the bowl.

6. Unscrew the battens and your slab is ready to go! You can keep the mould to use again if you wish.

A miniature pond is made in the same way as a large round pot. You will need to reinforce the sides to ensure that your pond will last. If you are making a pond, drill small holes for the pump's tubing at the pond's sides and then seal them tightly with silicone, or alternatively, hang the tube over the pond's edge, concealing it behind an attractive plant.

YOU WILL NEED: fine concrete, two large yet different sized plastic tubs, mesh for reinforcement, boards, oil, a paintbrush, a trowel, a piece of timber, weights, gloves, a stone or a file and possibly a pump, a drill and some silicone sealant.

1. Begin by oiling the inside of the larger tub and the outside of the smaller one.

2. Mix the concrete and fill the base with a concrete layer that is about 5 cm (2 in.) thick and pack it down. Place the smaller mould on top of the wet concrete, using a weight to keep it in place.

3. Insert the reinforcement mesh between the moulds and fill the remaining space with concrete. Tamp the concrete down with a piece of timber to get rid of any air bubbles and to level its surface.

4. Once the concrete has set, about 4 days, carefully remove the tubs.

5. Smooth away any sharp edges with a stone or a file.

6. If you would like to drill holes for a pump, use a masonry drill bit and seal the hole well with silicone sealant after feeding the pump's tubes through. Water pumps are available from DIY stores and other suppliers.

This method can be used to cast a small table, a planting bench or even a barbecue-cum-outdoor-kitchen. The only difference in casting the latter is that a hole is needed in the slab for a barbecue to fit through. Bear in mind too that the finished slab will be heavy, so it is a good idea to cast it close to where you would like to use it.

YOU WILL NEED: fine concrete, chipboard or film-faced plywood, timber battens, your barbecue's grill, a pencil, mesh for reinforcement, styrofoam, screws, a screwdriver, oil, a paintbrush, a trowel or a spatula, gloves, a stone or a file.

1. Begin by cutting the board and timber to your desired size and screwing your mould together. Oil the mould.

2. Use your barbecue's grill as a template for the hole in the slab. Draw an outline of it on the styrofoam and cut it out.

3. Oil your styrofoam cut-out and position it in the mould where you would like the barbecue to fit. Use a weight to keep the cut-out in place. Mix the concrete. Pour a thin layer of concrete into the mould.

4. Add the reinforcement mesh and top up with more concrete. Level the concrete's surface.

5. Cover the slab with plastic to help it retain moisture and to stop the concrete drying out too quickly. Leave the concrete to set for 3 days before removing the timber battens, then leave for another 3 days or so.

6. Finished! Smooth away any sharp edges with a stone or a file.

Making a starfish dish

With plenty of sand moulds and bowls available, there is no end to the possibilities for themed, little water features. To create this one, we used a starfish mould and a plastic bowl. This is an ideal project for beginners.

YOU WILL NEED: fine concrete, a plastic bowl, a sand mould, a weight, oil, a paintbrush, a trowel and a stone or a file.

1. Oil the inside of the plastic bowl and the outside of the mould.

2. Mix the concrete. Fill the bowl with concrete to about 2 cm (1 in.) below the top. This will stop the concrete overflowing when you add the mould.

3. Shake the bowl to get rid of any air bubbles and to level the concrete's surface. Gently press the sand mould into the wet concrete.

4. Put a weight on top of the smaller mould to stop it rising.

5. Leave the concrete to set for 24 to 48 hours, depending on the feature's size, then carefully remove the moulds. Smooth away any sharp edges with a stone or a file.

6. Fill with water for a small, elegant water feature.

A glass pendant is a particularly effective design feature that can be used to decorate the base of a concrete bowl. Mosaic tiles, broken pieces of porcelain or a small mirror are all objects that can also be used in this way.

YOU WILL NEED: fine concrete, two different sized bowls, a pendant (or another decorative feature), a thin piece of timber, a weight, oil, a paintbrush, a trowel and a stone or a file.

1. Begin by oiling the inside of the larger bowl and the outside of the smaller one.

2. Mix the concrete. Pour a 3 cm (1½ in.) layer of concrete into the base of the larger bowl. Shake the bowl gently to level the concrete and to find the exact centre of your bowl's base.

3. Position the pendant in the centre and press it down gently.

4. Place the smaller bowl on top, centre it and use a weight to hold it in place.

5. Fill the remaining edge space with concrete. Tamp the concrete down carefully using a thin piece of timber, so as not to get concrete under the small bowl and over the pendant.

6. Gently tap the larger bowl to level the surface and remove any air bubbles. Leave to set for 48 hours before removing the moulds and smoothing away any sharp edges with a stone or a file.

Making a stencilled stool

Stencils are an easy way to add colourful, attractive designs to concrete. You can create your own designs using adhesive figures and spray paint. We made a stool and used an adhesive flower wall stencil as a template for the pattern.

YOU WILL NEED: fine concrete, a plastic bucket, oil, a paintbrush, a stencil and spray paint.

1. Oil the inside of the plastic bucket thoroughly.

2. Mix the concrete. Fill the bucket with concrete to the desired height of the stool. Shake the bucket to get rid of any air bubbles and to level the concrete's surface.

3. Once the concrete has set (about 3 days), tip the bucket up and remove it.

4. Attach your chosen template to the stool, remembering that it will be the areas around the stencil that are painted.

5. Spray the stool with the paint, applying an even coat.

6. When the paint is dry, remove the template and the pattern will be revealed.

Making a natural impression

Nature offers us the most beautiful designs with which to make impressions in concrete—a simple tile with a leaf impression makes a fine piece of artwork for the garden. To ensure that the impression is clear, it is important to press the leaf firmly into the concrete. This method can also be used to decorate stepping stones.

YOU WILL NEED: fine concrete, a rectangular plastic tub, leaves, oil, a paintbrush, a trowel, small stones and a stone or a file.

1. Oil the mould and the underside of the leaf.

2. Mix the concrete and spread it out in the mould. We made our tile 3 cm (1½ in.) thick.

3. Shake the tub to get rid of any air bubbles and to ensure a smooth, level surface. Decide where the leaf should go.

4. Place the leaf in position, keeping it underside down on the concrete. Press down carefully.

5. Cover the leaf with small stones to create a clear, deep impression. Leave to set.

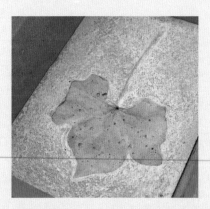

6. Wait 48 hours before removing the leaf and the mould. Smooth away any sharp edges on the tile with a stone or a file.

Making a leaf-shaped dish

A tightly packed mound of grit or coarse sand dampened with water makes a steady base for casting a leaf-shaped dish or bowl. Get out into the garden or ramble through the countryside to find a good leaf to use as a mould. We chose a giant hosta leaf for this project.

YOU WILL NEED: fine concrete, grit or coarse sand, water, a leaf, oil, a paintbrush, a nail, a trowel, gloves and a stone or a file.

1. Start by building a mound of grit or sand that is roughly the same shape as the leaf and dampen it to make it firm.

2. Place the leaf on the mound of grit or coarse sand underside up so its veins are showing. Oil the leaf.

3. Mix the concrete and cover the leaf with an even layer of it. Try to keep an eye on where the edges of the leaf are, helping to ensure a neater finish.

4. Pack concrete all over the leaf. Stick a nail into the concrete to ensure that it has a uniform thickness all over.

5. Leave the concrete to set for 4 to 5 days, depending on the size of your project. Remove the leaf carefully and file down the dish's edges.

6. The leaf should have left a clear impression in the concrete, making a pretty dish or water feature.

There are plenty of pretty mosaic tiles around to choose from, or alternatively, you could just make a plain birdbath. The general principle is the same and you can vary the shape of the hollow and the edge patterns as much as you like.

YOU WILL NEED: fine concrete, plywood, timber battens, mosaic tiles, an interior mould, screws, a screwdriver, oil, a paintbrush, a trowel, gloves and a stone or a file.

1. Begin by assembling the timber battens and plywood into a square mould by screwing the battens to the plywood in a square formation. The birdbath here measures 35 cm × 35 cm (14 in. × 14 in.). Oil the square mould and interior mould.

2. Mix the concrete. Fill the mould with it, packing the concrete down well. If you are wearing gloves, do this with your hands. Otherwise, use a trowel.

3. Place the interior mould in the middle of the concrete and press it down.

4. Put a weight in or on top of the interior mould to stop it rising.

5. Using your mosaic tiles, create any design you like around the edge. Press the tiles carefully down into the concrete.

6. Leave the birdbath to set for 2 days before removing the interior mould and the timber battens. Dampen it with water and leave to dry for another 2 days, then smooth away any sharp edges with a stone or a file.

Making a large round birdbath or a table top

A large plastic tub is the ideal mould for a large round birdbath or table top. We used a plastic serving dish to make the birdbath pattern here, but you can just as easily use one or a number of rubber balls. With a smooth finish, this project is perfect as a small, round table top. Be sure not to make your birdbath or table top too thin, as this can lead to cracking.

YOU WILL NEED: fine concrete, a large plastic tub, a decorative mould, oil, a paintbrush, a trowel, gloves and a stone or a file.

1. Start by oiling the bottom of the plastic tub and part way up the sides.

2. Fill the bottom of your mould with concrete up to about 8 cm (4 in.). Shake the tub to get rid of any air bubbles and to level the concrete's surface.

3. Oil the underside of the decorative mould.

4. Place the plastic mould in the centre of the tub and press down gently. Use small weights to keep the mould in position.

5. Leave to set for 4 days before removing the decorative mould.

6. Carefully lift the birdbath out of the tub and smooth away any sharp edges with a stone or a file.

Making a round birdbath

A round birdbath is relatively easy to make, especially when using a cardboard tube cut to size and a plastic lid for moulds. A large, round, plastic container would also work as an alternative to a plastic lid. Remember that the birdbath needs to be a few centimetres deep to last and to hold water. Our birdbath measures 25 cm (10 in.) in diameter.

YOU WILL NEED: fine concrete, a cardboard tube, a plastic lid, a piece of board, a ruler, a saw, oil, a paintbrush, a trowel or a spatula and a stone or a file.

1. Begin by sawing a 5 cm (2½ in.) ring from the cardboard tube. Place the ring on your piece of board. Oil the ring, the board and the plastic lid.

2. Mix the concrete. Fill the mould almost to the top with concrete. Shake the mould gently to distribute the concrete evenly and to get rid of any air bubbles.

3. Place the plastic lid in the centre and press it down carefully. Leave to set.

4. After 48 hours, the concrete should have set. Remove the plastic lid.

5. Remove the cardboard ring. If the ring does not come off easily, carefully cut it away.

6. Smooth away any sharp edges with a stone or a file.

Silicone moulds

Using silicone moulds is an excellent project for beginners. We found this great rose muffin case in a kitchen shop. The mould is extremely easy to use because silicon is flexible and will release the hardened concrete without any problems.

YOU WILL NEED: fine concrete, a silicone mould, oil, a paintbrush, a spatula and a stone or a file.

1. Begin by oiling the mould. Normally you don't need to oil silicone moulds, but we do just to be on the safe side.

2. Mix the concrete. Fill the moulds up to the top and skim off any excess using your spatula.

3. Shake the mould gently to distribute the concrete evenly and to get rid of any air bubbles. Leave to set on a flat surface.

4. After 24 hours, the concrete should have set and the roses will be ready to remove from the mould. Remove the roses and wash the mould afterwards if you would like to reuse it.

5. Smooth away any sharp edges with a stone or a file.

6. Arrange the roses prettily on a garden table or around a birdbath.

Making a heart with a split plastic mould

Split plastic moulds also work well with concrete, as they are easy to open once the heart has set solid, and you can reuse them! We found this split plastic heart mould in an art and craft shop.

YOU WILL NEED: fine concrete, a split plastic mould, oil, a paintbrush, a thin stick or a spatula and a stone or a file.

1. Oil the insides of both halves of the mould.

2. Mix the concrete. Pour the concrete into the mould and try to pack it down well to get rid of any air bubbles.

3. Leave the concrete to set for 24 hours before carefully opening the mould.

4. Lift the heart out of the mould.

5. Smooth away any of the heart's sharp edges with a stone or a file.

6. Don't worry if an imprint of the mould is left on the heart, as this will add to its charm.

Making a heart with a styrofoam mould

You can make any number of fun objects using styrofoam, like letters, flowers or even a birdbath. Styrofoam is available in many different thicknesses and is easy to draw on and cut, but remember to place the styrofoam on a flat surface before pouring in your concrete.

YOU WILL NEED: fine concrete, styrofoam, a piece of board, a pen, a serrated knife, weights, oil, a paintbrush, a trowel, gloves, a stone or a file.

1. Begin by sketching your design on the styrofoam. You can draw freehand or use a template. Cut out your design using a serrated knife.

2. Move the mould to the board. Oil the mould and the board.

3. Mix the concrete and fill the heart with it. Level the surface of the concrete.

4. Pack the concrete down and use your hands to make a hollow in the concrete. It is a good idea to wear protective gloves—ordinary washing up ones are suitable.

5. Neaten out the hollow, smoothing the surface. Leave to set for about 3 days.

6. Remove the heart carefully. Don't worry if the styrofoam breaks. Smooth away any sharp edges with a stone or a file.

This miniature birdbath can be made in a rectangular tub and is decorated here with a small heart-shaped relief, but the possibilities in terms of shape and design here are endless. Try using different moulds and shells to create something really special.

YOU WILL NEED: fine concrete, a rectangular tub, a bowl or a container, a small heart-shaped mould, weights, oil, a paintbrush, a trowel and a stone or a file.

1. Begin by oiling the inside of the rectangular tub and the outside of your bowl or container and heart-shaped mould.

2. Mix the concrete. Fill the base of the tub with concrete to about 8 cm (4 in.) deep. Shake the tub gently to level the concrete.

3. Push your bowl or container gently into the wet concrete. Put a weight in it to stop it from moving.

4. Position the heart-shaped mould where you would like it to be and press down gently.

5. Put a small weight on top of the heart-shaped mould as well. Leave to set for about 3 days.

6. Once the concrete has set, you can remove the moulds and smooth away any sharp edges with a stone or a file.

Making a garden bench

This is a slightly more advanced project that requires a good strong mould, some carpentry skills and a bit of patience, but it is not that difficult. Our bench is 115 cm (46 in.) long, 30 cm (12 in.) wide and 45 cm (18 in.) high, with the timber battens determining the thickness of the bench's legs. Cast this project upside down, with the seat at the bottom. Don't forget to reinforce it if you want it to last.

YOU WILL NEED: fine concrete, film-faced plywood, timber battens, mesh and rods for reinforcement, screws, a screwdriver, boards, oil, a paintbrush, a trowel and some gloves.

1. Start by cutting the parts of the exterior part of the mould to size and assembling them, leaving out the inside panels. Oil the mould.

2. Mix the concrete. Half fill the seat section with concrete, then pack it down and add the mesh for reinforcement. Fill with more concrete and level it.

3. Screw the inside panels to the inside of the mould. Fill the short sides with concrete, forming the legs of the bench.

4. Tamp the concrete down carefully with a piece of timber to get rid of any air bubbles, then reinforce the sides with reinforcing rods, using two for each leg.

5. Cover the bench with plastic to stop it setting too quickly and spray the bench with water over several days. Wait at least 4 days before removing the battens and inside panels.

6. To ensure that the bench will last, leave it for another week or so, and then move it out into the garden.

Making a tealight holder

These moulds, which are actually muffin cases, are great for making small, simple tealight holders. As the moulds are made of silicone, the finished holder never sticks and you can make a whole batch in one go. Use small or large tealights to make the hollows in the holders. Empty sour cream tubs also make fantastic moulds for this project.

YOU WILL NEED: fine concrete, small silicone moulds, oil, a paintbrush, a thin spatula and some tealights.

1. Begin by oiling the moulds. You technically don't need to oil silicone moulds, but we do to be on the safe side.

2. Oil the underneath and sides of the tealight.

3. Mix the concrete and fill the mould with it to just below the top, stopping the concrete from overflowing when you push in the tealight.

4. Shake the mould to get rid of any air bubbles and to level the concrete's surface.

5. Press the tealight into the centre of the concrete, then leave to set on a flat surface. It will take about 24 hours to set.

6. Carefully remove the holders from the moulds, and then wash the moulds so that they can be reused.

Making a board game

Silicone ice cube trays now come in a variety of shapes and sizes—there are stars, hearts, rings and plenty of other designs out there, although we have chosen to make a noughts and crosses, or tic-tac-toe, set here. This project can be a little fiddly but it is not difficult. You can also use the finished pieces as napkin weights if you wish.

YOU WILL NEED: fine concrete, ice cube moulds, oil, a paintbrush, a spatula, a square plastic container, tape and some spray paint.

1. Begin by oiling the ice cube moulds.

2. Mix the concrete. Fill the moulds and skim off the excess concrete. Shake the mould gently to distribute the concrete evenly and to get rid of any air bubbles.

3. Leave to set on a flat surface. Wait at least 24 hours before pressing out the pieces.

4. Use a square plastic container to make the board. Oil the inside of the container, then mix the concrete and pour a thin, 2 cm (1 in.) deep layer of it into the base of the mould. Leave to set for about 24 hours.

5. Turn out the concrete slab. Stick some tape on it to create a latticed pattern. Press the tape down firmly to stop the spray paint from getting in underneath it. Now apply the spray paint.

6. Once the paint is dry, remove the tape carefully. Use your concrete noughts and crosses as playing pieces.

Making a concrete cake

Using different moulds is a good way to vary the shape and appearance of cakes and other decorative objects that are made out of concrete. This project is almost as easy as making sandcastles at the beach!

YOU WILL NEED: fine concrete, a variety of cake-shaped moulds, oil, a paintbrush, a trowel or a spatula and a stone or a file.

1. Gather your cake-shaped moulds together.

2. Oil the inside of the moulds well.

3. Mix the concrete. Fill the moulds up to the top and skim off the excess concrete with your trowel or spatula.

4. Shake your mould to get rid of any air bubbles and leave to set on a flat surface.

5. The cakes should be ready after 24 to 48 hours, depending on their sizes. Carefully remove them from their moulds. Smooth away any sharp edges with a stone or a file.

6. The finished product. Transfer them to suitable holders and decorate all around with flowers.

Making an angel on a stake

Casting small angels is fairly straightforward—good angel moulds are available from most art and craft shops. If you would like to put the angel into a flowerbed or a pot, simply push a stake into the wet concrete to give it a raised position in the garden.

YOU WILL NEED: fine concrete, an angel mould, a zinc stake, oil, a paintbrush, a spatula, a stone or a file and an awl (optional).

1. Oil the mould and place it on a flat surface.

2. If you would like to add a stake to your angel, use an awl or a similarly sharp object to make a hole in the mould.

3. Mix the concrete and completely fill the mould with it—don't worry if it looks like you've put in too much.

4. Skim off the excess concrete and shake the mould to get rid of any air bubbles.

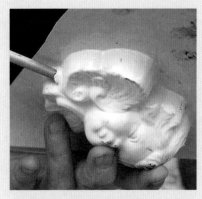

5. If you are planning on putting your angel on a stake, carefully insert the stake into the wet concrete now, then leave to set.

6. Remove the mould after 24 hours. Smooth away any sharp edges with a stone or a file.

Creating a beautiful concrete impression is simple—we used an angel Christmas decoration to make ours. To enhance the effect, we painted the angel silver. The paint will not last as long as the concrete, but it can easily be touched up.

YOU WILL NEED: fine concrete, a rectangular plastic container, an angel Christmas decoration (or whatever other object you would like to use), oil, a paintbrush, a trowel and some silver paint (optional).

1. Start by oiling the container and the angel.

2. Mix the concrete and spread it out in the container. We made our tile 3 cm (1½ in.) thick, but you can make yours thicker if you wish.

3. Shake the box to get rid of any air bubbles and to ensure a smooth, level surface.

4. Place the angel in the centre of the box and press down.

5. Leave to set for about 24 hours. Remove the angel carefully and wait another 24 hours.

6. Once the tile has set, paint the angel.

Making an angel

You can create your own mould for this project using silicone rubber and a porcelain angel figurine. Coat your chosen figurine with silicone rubber, available from art and craft shops, bearing in mind that it can take a little time and patience to get the mould just right. Next, stand the figurine in an old dish and apply about 10 coats of silicone rubber all over, leaving each coat to dry before applying the next one.

YOU WILL NEED: fine concrete, silicone rubber, a porcelain angel figurine, two paintbrushes, oil, a spatula, a bucket of sand and a stone or a file.

1. First, coat the figurine with silicone rubber, as detailed above.

2. Continue applying coats of silicone rubber, until you have applied around 10 of them.

3. Leave these to dry thoroughly, before carefully peeling off the silicone rubber mould.

4. Oil the mould, then stand it in a bucket of sand to keep it steady. Fully fill the mould with concrete and leave it to set.

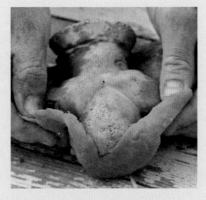

5. After 48 hours, the concrete should have set. Peel off the mould, or cut it off if necessary.

6. Smooth away any sharp edges with a stone or a file. Done!

Acknowledgments

We would like to thank
our wonderful families and
friends for their support,
encouragement and inspiration.

A special thank you to
master mason Niklas Nilsson.

Grateful thanks also to
our editor, Maria Ramdén,
for believing in our idea and
helping us along the way.